Symbols of Freedom

National Parks

Everglades National Park

M.C. Hall

Heinemann Library
Chicago, Illinois

Customer Service 888-454-2279
Visit our website at www.heinemannlibrary.com

Page layout by Ron Kamen and edesign
Photo research by Maria Joannou and Erica Newbery
Illustrations by Martin Sanders
Printed and bound in China by South China Printing Company Limited

10 09 08 07 06
10 9 8 7 6 5 4 3 2 1

Library of Congress Cataloging-in-Publication Data
Hall, Margaret, 1947-
  Everglades National Park / M.C. Hall.
     p. cm. -- (Symbols of freedom) (National parks)
  Includes bibliographical references and index.
  ISBN 1-4034-7795-7 (library binding : hardcover)
  1. Everglades National Park (Fla.)--Juvenile literature. I. Title. II. Series.
  F317.E9H35 2006
  917.59'39--dc22
                                 2005026571

Acknowledgments
The author and publishers are grateful to the following for permission to reproduce copyright material:
Alamy Images pp. **10** (Isifa Image Service s.r.o.), **11** (Florida Images), **14**, **15** (Andre Jenny), **16**, **20** (Byron Jorjorian), **26** (Robert Harding Picture Library Ltd), **27** (Dennis MacDonald); Corbis pp. **4** (Nik Wheeler), **5** (William A. Bake), **7** (Tony Arruza), **9** (Richard Cummins), **12** (David Muench), **18** (Tony Arruza), **19** (Dave G. Houser), **21** (Raymond Gehman), **22** (George McCarthy), **24** (Arthur Morris), **25** (Raymond Gehman); Digital Vision p. **23**; North Winds Pictures p. **8**; Randy Wells p. **13**; Superstock p. **17**.

Cover photograph of Everglades National Park reproduced with permission of Digital Vision.

Every effort has been made to contact copyright holders of any material reproduced in this book.
Any omissions will be rectified in subsequent printings if notice is given to the publisher.

Some words are shown in bold, **like this**. You can find out what they mean by looking in the glossary.

Contents

National parks are areas of land set aside for people to visit and enjoy. These parks do not belong to one person. They belong to everyone in the United States.

There are **388** national park areas in the United States. Everglades National Park is one of the largest. Most of the park is made up of grassy plants and water.

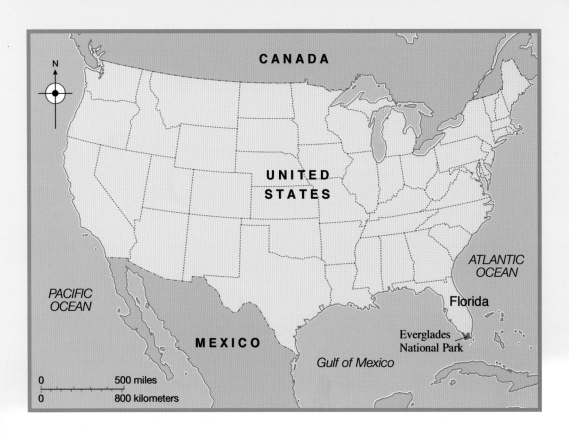

Everglades National Park is on the southern tip of Florida. The park includes many small islands and part of Florida Bay.

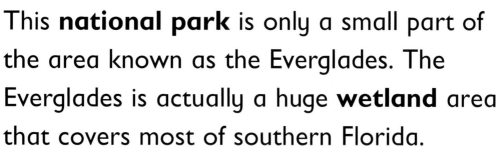

This **national park** is only a small part of the area known as the Everglades. The Everglades is actually a huge **wetland** area that covers most of southern Florida.

Water from Lake Okeechobee flows through the Everglades into the park.

The Everglades Long Ago

Native Americans were the first people of the Everglades. In the 1500s, **Spanish** explorers came for land and gold. Many natives were killed.

Later, a tribe called the Seminoles moved into the area.

People started to drain the **wetlands** to build farms and homes. In 1916, the **government** created a **state park** to protect some land. In 1947, a larger area was set aside as Everglades National Park.

Everglades Weather

There are two seasons in the Everglades. The **rainy season** lasts from May until November. The weather is hot and it rains every day. There are many huge thunderstorms.

The Everglades gets more rain in one thunderstorm than a desert gets in a year.

The **dry season** starts in December. The weather is usually warm. There is less rain and some water dries up.

This land is covered by water during the rainy season.

A River of Grass

Large areas of the Everglades are covered with sawgrass. This plant gets its name from the sharp edges of its leaves. It is not really a grass. It belongs to the sedge family.

In the **dry season**, the sawgrass turns from green to gold.

During the **rainy season**, the sawgrass is almost covered by water. From the air, it looks like a huge, green river. It can be as wide as a house in places.

The sawgrass is called a River of Grass.

Visiting Everglades National Park

People usually visit the Everglades during the **dry season**. More than one million people come to the park each year. Some come for just a day. Others camp overnight.

Chickee campsites let the wind blow through. They keep the campers cool and the insects away.

Visitors come to see the unusual plants and animals that live in the park. They also come to swim, hike, fish, and go boating.

Getting Around the Park

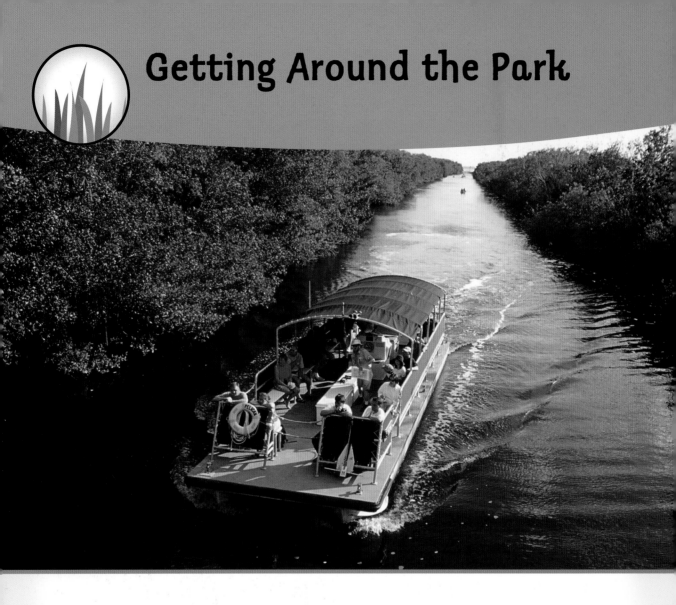

Some people explore the Everglades from boats. Others use canoes to travel along shallow rivers. Large boats also take visitors out into Florida Bay.

Visitors can also walk on wooden **boardwalks** that go over the **wetlands**. At Shark Valley, a trail leads to a tower where people can look out over the Everglades.

A tram carries passengers to this observation tower.

Beaches and Hammocks

There are sandy beaches along the southern part of the park. Visitors walk along the beaches to find the seashells that wash up there.

Sea turtles nest on the beaches.

Within the park there are small islands called **hammocks**. Thick forests of pine, mahogany, cypress, and palm trees grow there.

Strange Plants

Some strange trees grow in the Everglades. The gumbo-limbo has red bark that comes off in thin strips. The mangrove has roots that grow down into the water.

The gumbo-limbo is called the "tourist plant" because it looks like a visitor whose sunburn is peeling.

There are other odd plants in the Everglades. The roots of the strangler fig twist around other plants and choke them. The air plant does not need soil. It grows on trees with its roots in the air.

strangler fig

Endangered Animals

Crocodiles live in the park where the water is salty.

Everglades National Park is the only place in the world where both alligators and crocodiles live. The park is also home to other **endangered** animals, such as the Florida panther and sea turtles.

The manatee is a large animal that lives in warm, shallow water like Florida Bay. Visitors go out in boats hoping to see a manatee slowly swim by.

Manatees are also called sea cows.

Birds of the Everglades

Hundreds of different birds live in the Everglades. The brown pelican lives along the coast. It uses its big mouth like a net to catch fish.

Wading birds have long thin legs and sharp beaks.

Wading birds such as herons, egrets, and storks also live in the park. They walk through the shallow water looking for fish and frogs to eat.

Park Buildings and People

There are five visitor centers in Everglades National Park. Some of the visitor centers have displays that tell visitors about the plants, **wildlife**, and history of the park.

visitor center

Park rangers teach the public and tell visitors about the plants and animals. Some rangers even take visitors off the trails to see where alligators live.

Map of Everglades National Park

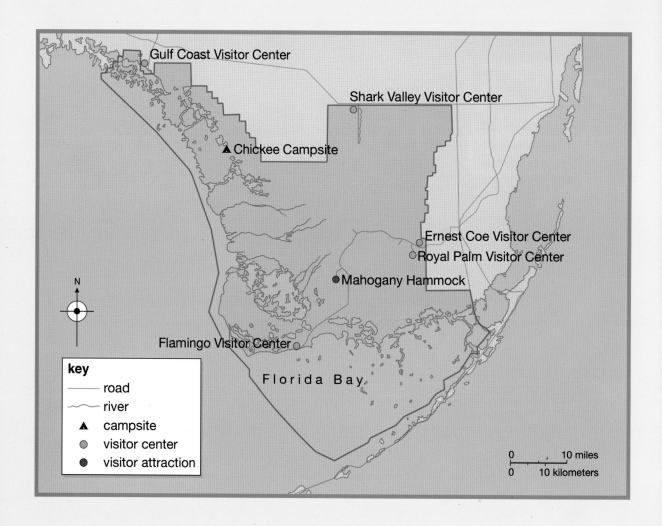

Gulf Coast Visitor Center

Shark Valley Visitor Center

Chickee Campsite

Ernest Coe Visitor Center
Royal Palm Visitor Center
Mahogany Hammock

Flamingo Visitor Center

Florida Bay

N

key
road
river
▲ campsite
○ visitor center
● visitor attraction

0   10 miles
0   10 kilometers

Timeline

Before 1500	Native American tribes live in the Everglades.
1500s	Spanish Explorers arrive in Florida.
1817–1858	The Seminoles and the United States **government** go to war over land.
1916	Royal Palm State Park is created to protect part of the Everglades.
1931	More of the Everglades is protected as **state park** land.
1947	Everglades National Park is established.
1979	The Everglades are named as a World Heritage Site.
1987	The Everglades are named a Wetland of International Interest.

Index